D0575953

1992

This book belongs
to
Jo Ellen and Lori Troydell

with lots of love
from Grammy

— enjoy your
own garden
&

maybe Mikie
can help you.

THE SECRET GARDEN

Notebook

A First Gardening Book

ILLUSTRATED BY
GRAHAM RUST

GODINE

For David

Illustrations copyright © 1991 by Graham Rust
Text and design copyright © 1991 by Breslich & Foss

First U.S. edition published in 1991 by
David R. Godine, Publisher, Inc.
Horticultural Hall
300 Massachusetts Avenue
Boston, Massachusetts 02115

Conceived and produced by Breslich & Foss, London

All rights reserved. No part of this book may be used or reproduced
in any manner whatsoever without written permission except in the case of
brief quotations embodied in critical articles and reviews.

Library of Congress Cataloging-in-Publication data available

ISBN: 0-87923-890-9
Designed by Peartree Design Associates
Original text by Judy Martin
Typeset by Chapterhouse
Printed and bound in Hong Kong

Contents

INTRODUCTION

The story of *The Secret Garden* unfolds layer upon layer, like a flower opening out its petals from a tightly closed bud. It begins with a bad-tempered little girl, Mary Lennox, making a long journey to a strange place – Misselthwaite Manor on the Yorkshire Moors – where at first she feels friendless and alone. Then Mary finds a secret garden, hidden away for years behind high walls, and a startlingly different life begins for her that leads to new interests and friendships and brings an unforeseen flowering of health and happiness.

All the changes occur because of the secret garden. Mary's story, and that of her friends Dickon and Colin, is woven together with wonderful descriptions of the garden waking from winter sleep and coming into new life through spring and summer. As the mysterious greyness of the winter garden breaks into the green shoots, buds and leaves of spring, the story evokes the fascination of all things that live and grow and go through changes.

The excitement of watching plants grow and seeing the different stages of growth, from the first new shoots to the full flush of beautiful flowers, is available to everyone. You do not need to have a proper garden – just a windowsill or a sunlit shelf is enough space to grow flowering plants, or even a few vegetables.

This book
looks at all the
pleasures that
Mary, Dickon
and Colin
discovered in
their secret
garden and
explains simply how you can get
the same sort of enjoyment through
gardening projects of your own.
You can adapt them to the amount
of space you can find for making
things grow in your own outdoor garden, or you can
use plant pots or window boxes to make little planting
spaces wherever you have room to put them – outside a
window, on a porch, beside the doorstep, or on a patio or
balcony.

Throughout the book, there are decorative notebook
pages where you can write down the progress of your
projects. The illustrations will help you to recognise
different kinds of plants and flowers, and the signs of the
seasons such as those described in the story of Mary,
Dickon and Colin in *The Secret Garden*.

The Garden in Spring

*The long warm rain had done strange
things to the herbaceous beds which bordered
the walk by the lower wall.
There were things sprouting and pushing out from
the roots of clumps of plants and there were
actually here and there glimpses of royal purple
and yellow unfurling among the stems of crocuses.
Six months before Mistress Mary would
have seen nothing of how the world was waking
up, but now she missed nothing.*

SIGNS OF SPRING

Mary Lennox made a long journey from her first home in India to Misselthwaite Manor on the English moors. Finding the secret garden, locked away untended for years, sent her on an even more exciting voyage of discovery. When she first entered the mysterious garden, it was a wintry brown, with bare stems and strange tangles of leafless plants. But Mary had found the garden just as spring was beginning, and she was soon to see many signs of new life breaking through in the neglected beds.

In spring, every kind of plant puts out new shoots and tiny leaves, waking up from winter dormancy, the period when a garden seems to sleep through the cold weather and short, sunless days. Among the first things Mary found were green points pushing up through the earth – the new leaves of bulbs growing underground. She thought the dried-out rose stems were dead, but Dickon soon showed her the living green wood that would put forward new growth, first leaves and then, eventually, colourful and fragrant flowers.

As the weather grew warmer and sunnier, all sorts of green things appeared in every corner of the garden. Together, Mary and Dickon discovered the wonders that the garden had to offer, often accompanied by the lively robin who had shown Mary the key to the secret garden.

The Green Points

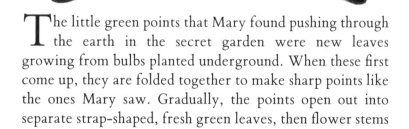

As she came near the second of these alcoves she stopped skipping. There had once been a flowerbed in it, and she thought she saw something sticking out of the earth – some sharp little pale green points. She remembered what Ben Weatherstaff had said, and she knelt down to look at them. 'Yes, they are tiny growing things and they might be crocuses or snowdrops or daffodils,' she whispered.

The little green points that Mary found pushing through the earth in the secret garden were new leaves growing from bulbs planted underground. When these first come up, they are folded together to make sharp points like the ones Mary saw. Gradually, the points open out into separate strap-shaped, fresh green leaves, then flower stems start to grow up through them and finally the brightly coloured petals of the spring flowers appear.

Many beautiful flowers grow from a bulb-shaped root. This bulb is a storage system for roots, leaves and flowers. Among the earliest flowers of spring are colourful crocuses in yellow, white or purple, and delicate white snowdrops with their tiny bell-like, hanging heads. Another pretty little flower is the grape hyacinth, with its vivid blue flowerheads. All of these flowers grow from quite small bulbs.

Larger bulbs produce larger flowers. Daffodils and narcissi form their familiar trumpet-shaped flowers on long stems, in all shades of yellow and orange. Later in spring, hyacinths come into bloom. These have heavy heads of small clustered florets, in blue, purple, red, pink, yellow or white. Tulips flower from late spring into summer. There are many different kinds, with smooth or frilled petals, in a range of strong colours from sunshine-yellow to red, pink and mauve, to a deep purple that is almost black.

Although no one had looked after the garden for years, the bulbs survived easily in the secret garden. This is because bulbs not only continue to produce new shoots year after year but also make their own new little bulbs, gradually forming more flowers.

Planting Spring Bulbs

Bulbs can be grown in flowerbeds or in the open ground. You can even let them grow up through a lawn or a patch of rough grass, like the ones in the secret garden that had continued to push up through the overgrown garden floor. If you do not have a garden with plenty of space like Mary's, you will find that bulbs are wonderful plants for window boxes and pots, and can be grown indoors as well as out.

Bulbs are planted out in autumn to give them time to develop well for spring. You can buy bulbs from your local garden centre or market. Some times they are sold in little packets printed with a picture of the flowers, or you can buy them singly, a few at a time, to get a mixture of colours.

Planting bulbs outdoors

All you need to do is make a hole in the earth and push the bulb down into it. A bulb has a flat base and a pointed tip. Plant the bulb with the tip sticking upwards and cover it with soil. Small bulbs such as crocuses, snowdrops and grape hyacinths, are planted about 7cm (3in) deep. The large bulbs of daffodils, hyacinths and tulips should be planted about 15cm (6in) deep.

Planting bulbs in pots

When you plant bulbs in pots, you can space them quite close together and they should be planted less deeply than in the ground. You can buy a special soil from a garden centre, called bulb fibre, to fill a bulb bowl, or you can plant the bulbs in a pot or window box using ordinary potting soil. Do not use garden soil in containers, as it may contain worms or bugs that will damage the bulbs.

Put the fibre or potting soil into the container, plant the bulbs with the tips about 2.5cm (1in) from the pot rim and then cover them up. Keep the pot moist, cool and shaded until the green points appear. You can put it on a balcony or windowsill, for example. If the weather is very cold, the bulbs can be protected by putting the pot into a black plastic bag. If you want the bulbs to flower indoors, do not bring them into a warm room until the leaf shoots have appeared.

Notebook

Use these pages to keep a note of the names of the bulbs that you plant, when the green points come up, and when the flowers appear. You could note down the flower colours, too.

I planted (bulb names)	on (date)	in (garden or pot)
tulip bulb	~ Feb 20/93	grn plastic pot

The green points
appeared on

The flowers
came out on

Mar 7

The Flowers of Spring

Most of the earliest spring flowers grow from bulbs planted underground, but as spring unfolds and the weather gets warmer, other flowers begin to appear.

Shrubs, which are woody, bushy plants, survive the winter well and several types quickly produce bright-coloured blooms when spring arrives. Forsythia brings out bright yellow, spiky flowers on bare branches, even before its leaves appear, as does the early-flowering honeysuckle, whose pretty, raggedy, white flowers are very fragrant. The flowering quince produces brilliant scarlet, saucer-shaped flowers.

If you do not have the space to grow shrubs, you can grow flowers on plants that climb upwards. Clematis is a family of lovely climbing plants that ramble and trail across fences and walls, clinging on with their own tendrils. Some clematis flower in spring, others in summer and autumn. The flower colours range from white to delicate pale pink to velvety, deep purple.

When the cold weather is over, smaller, softer plants appear. There are many small, low-growing plants that form hummocks or spreading mats of leaves creeping over the earth, and these will become studded with tiny jewel-like flowers through spring and summer. These plants include alyssum, saxifrage, alpine pansies and double

daisies. As
the spring
becomes
warmer,
larger plants
develop their new
leaves and flowers. Anemones
are cheerful spring flowers with beautiful strong colours –
white, red and blue. Aquilegia, which Dickon called by its
common name of columbine, produces delicately shaped
flowers with a trumpet-like centre surrounded by fine
petals with long spurs. Some columbines are single-col-
oured – white, yellow, mauve and blue – while others have a
trumpet of one colour and outer petals of another colour.

In the secret garden, Mary and Dickon also found tall
irises. These have a type of root system called a rhizome.
Like bulbs, rhizomes live underground through the winter
and produce new leaves and flowers in spring. Irises come
in the same beautiful colours as columbines, but the large
flowers are quite different in shape. Two sets of petals grow
from the flower centre. The top petals curl up and over, the
lower ones hang gracefully downwards.

Wildflowers for the Garden

The gardens of Misselthwaite Manor opened out onto the moors, where many types of flowers were growing wild in the open countryside. Wildflowers multiply by scattering their seeds, which can be carried by the wind or by birds or small animals to different places where new plants will then grow and flower. No doubt even the secret garden, protected by its high walls, contained wildflowers that had come there by chance and started to grow among the garden plants.

You can grow wildflowers from seed in your garden by buying packets of seed for individual flowers or for mixed flower groups. Usually they will grow quite easily if you scatter the seed into the garden bed. There will be notes on the seed packet telling you how and when to sow them, so read these carefully.

Corn marigold
Bright yellow daisy-like flowers carried upright on long, leafy stems.

Cowslip
Clustered heads of small yellow flowers on strong, upright stems above low-growing rosettes of fresh green leaves.

Field poppy
Brilliant scarlet, large flowers growing on tall, arching stems.

Feverfew
Clusters of daisy-like white and yellow flowers on long, branching stems. The plants are sweet-smelling.

Knapweed
The large, shaggy-petalled purple-pink flowers of this tall plant are very attractive to butterflies and bees.

Toadflax
This is another tall plant that carries small snapdragon-type flowers that are bright yellow tipped with orange.

Wild pansy
A tiny, delicate version of the pansy, with petals flushed white, yellow, pink and violet.

Wild primrose
Delicate short-stemmed, saucer-shaped flowers of primrose-yellow nestle among fresh green leaves.

TIDYING THE GARDEN
IN SPRING

Mary and Dickon found plenty of work to do in the secret garden because it had been growing wild for so many years, but every garden needs some attention in spring, because some of the leaves and branches will have died during the winter and rain or snow may have made the garden muddy and rough. Here are some jobs you can do in the garden while the plants are developing their new life.

Clearing leaves
Dead leaves left over from the autumn may still be lying on the ground. You can clear paths and flowerbeds of this loose covering – a short-handled rake is a useful tool for this job. You should also remove any old browned and rotted leaves left on the plants.

Weeding
Mary had to clear the soil around the new spring bulbs pushing up through the earth. You too may find that in parts of your garden grass and weeds are choking the newly developing garden plants. Some weeds pull up easily, especially if the earth is damp, but you may need a trowel to dig out the more deeply rooted weeds.

Digging
After months of rain, frost and snow, the soil in the garden gets beaten down and muddy. Turning over the top layers of soil with a garden fork is an important task, especially if you plan to put new young plants into the flowerbeds later in the spring. The ground needs to be opened up and made loose. Take out any big stones and break up the solid chunks of mud.

Pruning
When Mary showed Dickon the roses in the secret garden, she

did not know if they were alive or dead, because some of the branches were grey and broke easily. To tidy up plants such as roses, shrubs and fruit trees you can cut off long stems and dead branches, but first you should ask someone who, like Dickon, knows how the plants grow to help you to decide which stems to cut. Use proper garden clippers, not scissors. If the rose stems are prickly, you may need to wear gloves.

Notebook

Write down the jobs you plan to do in the garden and make a note of when you finish them.

Job to do
(weeding, digging)

Part of garden
(lawns, paths, beds)

Job completed
(day and date)

_____   _____   _____

_____   _____   _____

_____   _____   _____

_____   _____   _____

_____   _____   _____

_____   _____   _____

As you work in the garden, look for signs of spring and write down what you see, such as new plants emerging, fresh buds opening on woody stems, birds building nests. If you do not have a garden of your own, watch out for the same things in a park or the nearby countryside.

New plants	Green buds	Birds and animals

The Garden in Summer

*They always called it Magic, and indeed it seemed
like it in the months that followed – the wonderful
months – the radiant months – the amazing ones.
Oh the things which happened in that garden . . .
At first it seemed that green things would
never cease pushing their way through the earth,
in the grass, in the beds, even in the crevices
of the walls. Then the green things began
to show buds, and the buds began to unfurl and
show colour, every shade of blue, every shade
of purple, every tint and hue of crimson.*

SUMMER MAGIC

After the first exciting rush of spring, the garden seems to pause for a time, as if gathering its energy. Then comes the magic period of summer when new things occur every day. This was the magic that Colin felt in the secret garden as it burst into life and colour. The pleasure of the garden made Colin well after his long years as an invalid. Colin, Mary and Dickon all gained strength and happiness from the magical regrowth of the plants.

Many garden plants are at their finest in summer. Trees and shrubs are clothed with colourful leaves, and many produce beautiful flowers during the warmer months. Roses are one of the spectacular sights of summer, as Mary found when the old climbing roses spread their new blooms all over the secret garden.

All sorts of different plants produce brilliant summer displays. There are soft, cushiony plants that creep along the ground and become studded with tiny dots of colour. There are plants with pretty leaves in all shapes and sizes, among which the flowers are half-concealed. And there are tall, strong plants that produce long spikes and nodding clusters of flowers standing proudly above the multi-coloured growth in the flowerbeds. Between the beds, the grass grows thick and lush, making a solid green carpet for the garden floor.

Mary and Dickon's
Flower Garden

They sat down and he took a clumsy little brown-paper package out of his coat pocket. He untied the string and inside there were ever so many neater and smaller packages, with a picture of a flower on each one. There's a lot o' mignonette and poppies,' he said. 'Mignonette's the sweetest smellin' things as grows an' it'll grow wherever you cast it, same as poppies will. Them as'll come up and bloom if you just whistle to 'em, them's the nicest of all.'

Within the secret garden many plants were growing that had quietly been renewing themselves year after year while no one visited the garden. As Mary and Dickon set to work in the garden, tidying the ground, weeding the beds and uncovering the earth, they found many treasures all ready to create new colour for the spring and summer. However, Mary also wanted to grow plants of her own in the garden, so Dickon brought her packages of seeds that would quickly grow into new plants and produce brilliant flowers.

Many of the most beautiful flowers of summer belong to plants called annuals. These plants are grown from seed each year and produce all their leaves and flowers only a few weeks after the seeds are put into the earth. You can sow seeds directly into the garden once the weather becomes fine and warm in mid to late spring. If you do not have a garden, or even a small flowerbed, you can still grow flowers in trays and pots, in window boxes, tubs or hanging baskets. All summer long you can have colour and scent from plants that you have grown yourself from seed.

Flowering plants, like the ones that had been growing all along in the secret garden, are called perennials – this means that they come up and flower again every year. Perennial plants are sold at garden centres as young plants during spring and early summer. If you want to buy perennial plants, find out how large they will eventually become. You can grow tall or spreading plants in garden beds, but if you want to grow them in pots or troughs, you need to choose small to medium-sized plants.

GROWING FLOWERS FROM SEED

When you buy seeds, look at the picture on the front of the packet to see what the flowers will be like. You should also check the instructions on the back of the packet to find out when and where to sow the seeds and when the plants will flower. You can start your sowings from early spring onwards.

Sowing seeds
When the spring weather becomes fine and warm, and there is no danger of frost, you can sow seeds directly into the ground outdoors. Scatter them thinly on the flowerbed and cover them very finely with soil.

If you have no garden, or you want to sow your seeds early in the season and then plant them outdoors later, you can sow them in a seed tray or pot. Buy a bag of fine potting soil for seed-sowing at a garden centre.

Fill the tray or pot with this soil and then moisten it. Sow the seeds thinly on the surface and cover them very lightly.

When the seedlings appear, make sure they get plenty of light by keeping the tray on a brightly lit windowsill, but take care that they are not scorched by strong sun if the weather becomes very warm. Water the soil gently to keep it moist.

Pricking out seedlings

Each seed first sends up two little rounded leaves, then each plant's proper leaves begin to develop.

When the seed-lings have two or three pairs of leaves, you need to thin them out so that they are less crowded and have more room to grow. To do this you must dig up every other seedling and plant it somewhere else. Dig the seedlings up gently, taking care not to damage their tender roots.

Hold the top of the seedling gently and use a small stick or trowel to lever up the roots. Make a hole in the soil where you want to put the plant and carefully lower the roots into the hole. Then gently press the soil down around the base of the plant stem.

Seedlings growing in pots or trays can be moved to individual small pots. If they are in the garden, you can space them out more widely in the flowerbed.

FLOWERS TO GROW
FROM SEED

Busy lizzies
Fresh,
bushy
plants with
bright flowers
in a colour range from white
through shades of pink and red
to mauve and purple. Some have
striped petals.

Butterfly flower
These
flowers
have pretty,
freckled petals in pinks and
mauves. The bright green leaves
make lovely feathery shapes.

Cornflower
The tiny
petals are
clustered
into ruff-shaped
or ball-shaped
flowers. Blue cornflowers are
especially lovely, but there are
also pink and white varieties.

Larkspur
These are grand,
tall plants with long
flowerheads in
beautiful shades of
blue. They are best
suited to garden
planting and are
really too large for
pots or windowboxes.

Marigolds
The pretty,
feathery
leaves of
French marigolds help to show
off the masses of flowers which
come in all shades of brilliant
yellow and orange.

Mask flower
Bright scarlet,
small saucer-
shaped flowers are
carried on delicate
leafy stems that
spread and trail.

Mignonette

Sweet-scented, tufted, orange or red flowers are carried among slender, light green leaves.

Nemesia

These quick-growing plants have a range of bright colours – white, cream, yellow, orange, pink and red.

Petunia

The vivid trumpet-shaped flowers have plain-coloured or striped petals in white, yellow, red, pink or purple.

Poppy

Poppies are wonderful large saucer-shaped, brightly coloured flowers. The plants have pretty, ferny leaves and the stems grow very tall.

Sweet pea

These plants produce fine tendrils that will cling to fences, walls or bushes. They climb up from the flowerbed, showing off their delicate white, yellow, pink, red or purple flowers.

Verbena

These attractive trailing plants have long flower stems bearing clustered red or pink flowers with white centres.

Notebook

If you sow a lot of seeds, it is easy to forget what they are in the time between sowing the seed and seeing the seedlings coming up. To remind yourself, draw a map and keep a note below of the flower names and the times of sowing.

I sowed the seeds of (flower name)   on (date)

_____   _____

_____   _____

_____   _____

_____   _____

_____   _____

The seedlings appeared on (date)   The flowers came out on (date)

A Miniature Rose Garden

The secret garden was full of roses, because they had been the favourite flower of Colin's mother who had made the garden originally. Many people love to have roses in the garden – they are among the most beautiful flowers of summer. Rose bushes and climbing roses grow on year after year, producing more and more flowers.

Even if you do not have much room, you can grow miniature roses in pots or in a window box. Miniature rose bushes grow to between 15cm (6in) and 30cm (12in) high. There are lots of lovely colours to choose from – you will easily find white, pink or red flowers, and there are also creamy tints and orange shades. Some small roses have two colours in each flower, such as cream merging into pink.

When you are growing roses in containers, you need to plant them in good quality potting soil which you can buy by the bag at a garden centre. This soil is specially mixed to contain ingredients that provide nourishment for the plants. Roses should be grown out of doors – they need lots of light and fresh air around them. They also need plenty of water and you may need to water them every day during the summer. Make sure that your pot or trough has

holes in the
base to allow
the water to drain
through. Stand the con-
tainer in a tray if necessary.

The rose stems will become
bare during winter, like the roses in the
secret garden, but they will come to life again
each spring and make new buds and shoots. At this time you
should freshen the soil in the container. One method of
doing this is called top-dressing. This means that you take
out the top layer of old soil and put in a fresh layer. Every
second year, in early spring, take the roses out and replant
them in clean potting soil to give the plants a fresh start.
You can keep roses tidy by cutting the stems back very
early in spring before new buds have unfolded. Use garden
clippers and cut the stem just above a bud. Cut it at an
angle, sloping down and away from the bud. The stems
have sharp thorns so you will need to wear gloves.

Pruning encourages more flowers to grow. After the
rose has been pruned, it will put out lots of fresh new
shoots. Throughout the flowering season, cut the flowers as
they fade and die, so that new flower buds can form to take
their place.

MISTRESS MARY'S
BELLFLOWERS

'Are there any flowers that look like
bells?' she inquired.
'Lilies o' the valley does', he answered,
digging away with the trowel, 'an' there's
Canterbury bells an' campanulas.'
. . . Then Mary told him about Basil and his
brothers and sisters in India . . . 'They used
to dance round and sing at me. They sang:

"Mistress Mary, quite contrary,
How does your garden grow
With silver bells and cockle shells,
And marigolds all in a row."

I just remembered it and it made me
wonder if there were really flowers just
like silver bells.'

The children in India had teased Mary by calling her 'Mistress Mary, quite contrary', but in the secret garden her memory of the rhyme introduced her to new flower names – those of flowers that look like bells.

Lilies of the valley grow clumps of furling spear-shaped leaves. Their graceful arching flower stems appear in spring, and are hung with clusters of tiny white bells that have a sweet scent. They grow from strong underground roots called rhizomes. Once you have planted these rhizomes in the garden, they produce more and more flowers each year.

Canterbury bells are tall flower spikes with large bell-shaped flowers in white, pink or purple. There are several different types of campanulas that you can grow in the garden. Their bellflowers are white and shades of bright blue or blue-purple. Some have fine, trailing stems that carry a spreading mass of flowers. Others stand more upright and the flowers are clustered on their stems. You can grow campanulas from seed, or buy young plants from a garden centre in spring and early summer.

Some bulbs produce bell-like flowers. The flowers of fritillaries droop gracefully from the stems and have a pretty, lacy texture. They come in delicate shades of mauve or purple. You can plant the bulbs in pots or in a garden. Bluebells make a lovely sight growing wild in the woods in spring, but you can also buy bluebell bulbs for planting in the garden. They look especially pretty, making a carpet of colour under shrubs and trees, just as they do when they grow wild in the countryside.

A Windowsill Flower
Garden

A windowsill is an excellent place to grow flowers because you can see them from both inside and outside the house and they will make a bright feature even on dull days. You can plant them directly into potting soil in a trough or box, or you can grow the plants in individual pots and arrange the pots inside the box so that the flowers seem to be growing all together. You need to plan the arrangement carefully to get the heights, shapes and colours right.

First, think about the colours – do you want lots of different colours, or only shades of the same colour You might decide to have flowers that range from light to dark pink, for example, or all red flowers, or you could mix yellow, red, pink, blue and white flowers in the display. When you have decided which colours you want, you can choose the flower shapes and sizes.

Height and shape are important when you plant a window box. You must put the tallest plants with the largest leaves at the back of the box, then the slightly smaller plants, putting the smallest at the front so that they are not overshadowed by anything else. Trailing plants such as lobelia or ivy look lovely at the front of a window box, because they will grow over the edges and cascade down from the windowsill.

Make sure that the box sits securely on the window-sill and will not tip over or be blown off by the wind. If you do not have a suitable windowsill, there may be other places around the house or garden where you can put boxes of flowers, such as on a balcony or patio, on the steps by a door, or on a low garden wall.

New Plants from Old

Growing plants from seed is a good way to build up your stock of flowering plants, but once you have fully grown plants, there is another way that you can make more. You can grow them from stem cuttings. A cutting is a strong stem, with a few leaves and a healthy growing tip. If you cut it off the parent plant and put the cut end into a pot of moist soil, it will soon grow roots under the soil and then develop new stems, leaves and flowers.

The easiest plants to grow from cuttings are those with firm and quite thick stems. You need to use green stems, not woody brown ones as these do not root easily. Fuchsias are plants that produce both soft green and hard brown woody stems. If you take cuttings from a fuchsia use the newer green growth. Very fine-stemmed plants are not suitable for cuttings, as the stem may wither before it has time to make roots.

Geraniums are very quick to make new plants from stem cuttings. A cutting grows into a plant that looks exactly the same as the one it came from, so if you plant a cutting from a pink geranium, the new plant will have pink flowers too. Busy lizzies are also easy to grow in this way.

Use non-flowering stems for the cuttings; that is, leafy stems that are not bearing flowers or developing flower buds.

Taking a cutting

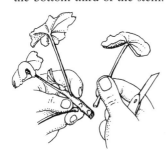

Choose a strong stem with a few open leaves and new leaf buds forming at the tip. Cut the stem just below a leaf and take off the lower leaves on the bottom third of the stem.

Fill a small plant pot with potting soil. Make a hole in the soil and push in the cut end of the stem. Firm the soil around the stem by pressing it down with your fingers.

Keep the soil moist and do not disturb the stem until you see new shoots and leaves start to grow. Then you can leave it to grow on in the same pot, or you can plant it out in the garden or put it into a hanging basket or window box.

PRESSED AND DRIED FLOWERS

Flowers look beautiful growing in the garden or in pots throughout spring and summer and into autumn. As the days get darker and the weather gets colder, however, you will see fewer flowers growing outdoors. To keep the prettiness of flowers through winter, you can preserve garden or wild flowers by pressing or drying them. You can make a dried-flower arrangement for your living room or bedroom, or you can make pictures and cards using pressed flowers.

You will need to experiment a bit with methods of drying and pressing different kinds of flowers, as they do change shape and colour as they dry out.

Pressing flowers

You need quite delicate, flatly formed flowers for pressing. Small flowers with soft petals and fine stems are most suitable.

Pick the flowers when they are fully open during the middle of the day in dry, sunny weather, not when the flowers are wet from rain or dew.

Lay the flowers on a sheet of soft, absorbent paper – you can use blotting paper or tissues.

Spread the stems and petals carefully as you lay the flowers down.

Put a clean piece of paper or tissue over the flowers and place the paper layers between the pages of a large book – a telephone directory is fine. Put another book on top of the first to weight it down.

Leave the flowers for a few days until they have flattened and dried out completely. Take them out of the paper gently, so that you do not damage the fine petals.

Drying flowers in sand

If you want to dry larger flowers or flower sprays with strong stems and leaves, you can put them into a box (a shoe box is suitable) with some dry sand.

The sand must be completely dry. Fill half of the box and place the flowers on the sand. Cover them gently with more sand, sprinkling it on so that it falls between the petals and leaves. Put the lid back on the box and leave it in a warm, dry room. It may take more than a week for the flowers to dry properly. When they are ready, take them out of the box and gently shake or brush off the loose sand.

Air drying

Tall flowers and thick, strong grasses can be dried by hanging them in the air. Make up a bunch of flower stems or grasses and tie the bottoms of the stems together with string. Hang the bunch upside down in a cool, dry, shady place indoors.

43

Food from the Garden

*The Secret Garden was not the only one
Dickon worked in. Round the cottage on the
moor there was a piece of ground enclosed
by a low wall of rough stones.
Early in the morning and late in the fading
twilight and on all the days Colin and
Mary did not see him, Dickon worked there
planting or tending potatoes and cabbages,
turnips, carrots and herbs for
his mother.*

Dickon's Vegetable Garden

Living in their cottage on the moors, miles from anywhere, Dickon's large family needed the produce from his vegetable garden in order to stay well fed, healthy and happy. Dickon was lucky in having a large patch of ground walled off from the surrounding moor, in which he could dig the earth and plant all sorts of vegetables, large and small.

Some of the vegetables that Dickon grew, such as potatoes, turnips and cabbages, need plenty of space to grow. They need room for their stems and leaves to spread out above ground, and for their roots to grow large and strong underground.

In modern gardens, especially in towns where gardens are often quite small, there may not be much room to grow vegetables – certainly not enough to feed a whole family all summer as Dickon did. However, there are several food plants that you can grow quite easily in a small garden bed, or even in pots if you have no patch of open ground. These include delicious fresh salad crops and fragrant herbs like those that Dickon grew for his mother to add to her cooking.

EASY-TO-GROW VEGETABLES

You can grow these vegetables from seed, and then plant them in a garden bed or in pots that can stand outdoors in a yard or on a patio or balcony. Vegetables can be grown indoors in pots if you keep them near a window and provide them with plenty of sunshine, fresh air and moisture, but they *do* need all these things to grow well. Especially, they need plenty of moisture to grow fresh and strong, so you must keep them well watered.

Lettuces

Lettuces grow from quite small seeds, so you should not sow all of the seeds in your packet at one time, or you will have far more lettuce than you can eat when it comes to harvest time. Sow just a few seeds in small pots, and prick out the seedlings (see page 29). If you sow a few more each month through spring and early summer you will go on growing fresh crops.

Tomatoes

You can sow these as seeds or buy young tomato plants in spring. As with lettuces, do not grow too many all at once. One plant produces lots of tomatoes.

Tomato plants grow quite tall and they need to be tied to canes so that they will stand upright. Yellow flowers appear before the tomatoes start to form. When four or five stems have flowered, pinch out new shoots and flower buds with your fingertips to stop further growth, otherwise the tomatoes that are already forming may remain rather small.

Radishes

Radish seeds are quite big, so space them out well when you

sow them. You should get a crop quite quickly (within about four weeks of sowing). You must supply plenty of water as the red radish roots swell under the soil by taking in moisture.

Runner beans

These make tall, rambly climbing plants which need something to climb up, such as a long cane, a fencepost, or strings tied to a fence that the stems can wrap around. The plants produce bright red flowers as pretty to look at as the beans are delicious to eat.

QUICK-GROWING SALADS

One of the easiest ways to grow food plants is to sprout fresh shoots from seeds. You can grow cress, which has crispy white shoots and tiny fresh green leaves, in just a few days from seed. Beans are also types of seed, and small green mung beans quickly produce delicious crunchy bean shoots. Both of these foods are very easy to grow in a dish or jar – you don't need to have a garden at all! Sprouted shoots are delicious in salads or sandwiches.

Growing cress

There are a lot of cress seeds in one packet and you may not need to use them all at once. Use a few at a time so that you can start a new crop of cress just as you are harvesting the shoots from the previous one.

To sow the seeds, put a layer of folded paper towels or tissues in the bottom of a shallow dish, dampen them with clean water and sprinkle on some seeds. Do not sow them too thickly – give them room to grow.

Place the dish in a cool, shady place and keep the layer of paper damp while the seeds are sprouting. As the shoots appear, move the dish to a lighter position, such as a windowsill.

It will take between three and six days for the shoots to grow long enough and form their little leaves. To harvest them, cut through the base of the shoots with kitchen scissors and discard the damp paper.

Sprouting mung beans

You can buy mung beans in a health food store and in some supermarkets. They are very small green beans that are hard and shiny.

Mung beans must be kept damp all the time they are sprouting. First, put the beans in a strainer and rinse them thoroughly under clean running water. Then put them into a bowl of water and let them stand overnight. This softens them ready for sprouting.

Drain off the beans and put them into a jar or plastic container. The bean shoots grow quite large, so put only a shallow layer of the wet beans in the bottom of the container, leaving plenty of room for the shoots to develop. Cover the top of the container with a piece of muslin or some other fine cloth, held in place with a rubber band.

You must rinse out the container with clean water twice a day, morning and evening, to keep the beans fresh while they sprout. Pour the water out through the cloth so that the beans do not escape or become damaged and keep the

cover on between rinsings.

Sprouting beans need gentle warmth. If you keep them in a place that is too hot or too cold they may become mouldy and then you cannot eat them. You should find that the shoots are ready to eat in just a few days. Use them quickly, while they are at their freshest.

Notebook

Keep a note of the vegetables that you grow – when you sowed the seed or planted the new plants, and how soon you were able to take a harvest from the plants.

I sowed seeds of (vegetable name)	on (date)	The seedlings came up on (date)

93 ① lettuce, Spinach, pole peans, radishes, carrots, beats,
② broc., cuc, cauliflower - too many of everything else - nev

I ate my first vegetables on
(date)

~~umpkin~~, Zuc., peppers, eggplant
~~on~~, just a couple seeds of each

A WINDOWSILL HERB GARDEN

Herbs are plants with edible leaves that have distinctive scents and tastes. Unlike lettuces or cabbages, the leaves are not eaten whole as a vegetable but are used to flavour and sweeten other foods.

There are many sorts of herbs with many uses. You can add the leaves to cooked foods, such as beef, lamb, chicken or turkey, omelettes, pies, stews and vegetables such as potatoes, peas and greens. Some are particularly good in cold dishes – in salads or sandwiches, or as a garnish for a snack to make it look and taste a little different. Some herbs give an extra light, clean taste to sweet dishes such as puddings and sauces, or to fresh fruits and cool drinks.

With gentle herbs, such as mint and lemon balm, you can use whole leaves to garnish and flavour your food. Others, such as chives and thyme, are stronger-tasting and it is better to chop the leaves and use just a little.

If you want the herbs that you grow to be handy when you are preparing food, you can make a herb garden on the kitchen windowsill. The herbs can grow outside while the weather is warm during spring and autumn, or you can keep the pots indoors by the window if it is more convenient. Like all plants, herbs grow best if they have plenty of light and fresh air.

Many of the herbs produce strong roots, so the easiest way to grow them is in individual pots. You can simply group these on the windowsill, or put them into a window box or trough. Make sure that you give them plenty of water, especially when the weather is dry.

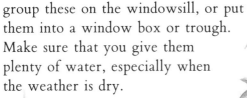

HERBS TO GROW IN POTS

These are a few of the easiest herbs to grow. You can start some of them from seed, but it is best to buy others as little plants from a garden centre. Once they are planted in a pot with some good potting soil, they will grow rapidly and give you lots of fresh leaves throughout the summer.

A plant that is filling its pot can be divided so that you get two plants from one. Take the plant out of the pot, gently pull apart the stems and roots down the middle, and plant the two halves in separate pots.

Chives

The long grassy leaves of chives have a slightly oniony taste that makes a very good flavouring for salads, sandwiches and fresh vegetables. Chop the leaves into small pieces and sprinkle them on food.

You can grow chives from seed sown in spring. Plant the seedlings in individual pots. Chives have pretty pink flowers in summer.

Lemon balm

The heart-shaped leaves of lemon balm are very fragrant. You can add them to cool drinks, cold desserts, fruit puddings and milky custards or sauces.

Start with a single, small plant and move it into a larger pot as it grows bushy.

Marjoram

This is a bushy little plant, growing up to 25cm (10in) high, with sweet-scented leaves that make excellent seasoning for meat and poultry.

Sow seed in spring and you will have plants for summer. You need only sow a few seeds in small pots, otherwise you will have many more plants than you can use. When the plants are well grown, flowers will appear, but you should take these off to encourage the plant to grow more leaves.

Mint

There are several different kinds of mint, such as spearmint, pepper-mint, applemint and pineapple mint. All of these have sweet-tasting minty leaves that go well with vegetables but also give a light, pleasant flavour to fruit salad or cool fruity drinks.

An easy way to start a stock of mint is to ask someone who already has mint plants to pull up a rooted stem for you, which you can plant in a pot. Mint spreads rapidly, so it needs a good-sized pot. In fact, you may need to divide the mint between two pots after it has been growing for some while.

Thyme

This small shrubby plant produces aromatic leaves that give a strong flavour in cooked dishes. There is also a variety called lemon thyme that goes well with light desserts and fruit drinks.

You can sow thyme seed in spring. As with marjoram, just sow a few seeds to begin with. When the plants have grown, take off any flower buds that appear, as these are no use for cooking and the plant will make more leaves if it does not come into flower.

Notebook

Note down the herbs that you grow from seeds – when you planted them and when you could first use the leaves.

Name of herb	Seeds sown (date)	leaves ready (date)

List all the herbs you are growing on your kitchen windowsill and the ways you have used them to flavour your food (write down whether it was a cooked dish, a salad, sandwich, dessert or drink).

Name of herb

I put the herb into (name of food)